D0926996

Literacy Consultants
DAVID BOOTH • KATHLEEN GOULD LUNDY

Social Studies Consultant
PETER PAPPAS

A Harcourt Achieve Imprint

10801 N. Mopac Expressway
Building # 3
Austin, TX 78759
1.800.531.5015

Steck-Vaughn is a trademark of Harcourt Achieve Inc. registered in the United States of America and/or other jurisdictions. All inquiries should be mailed to: Paralegal Department, 6277 Sea Harbor Drive, Orlando, FL 32887.

Ru'bicon © 2007 Rubicon Publishing Inc.
www. rubiconpublishing.com

Project Editor: Kim Koh
Editor: Vicki Low
Art Director: Jen Harvey
Project Designer: Jan-John Rivera

7 8 9 10 11   5 4 3 2 1

Fire Mountain
ISBN 13: 978-1-4190-3198-4
ISBN 10:   1-4190-3198-8

Printed in Singapore

PHOTO CREDITS: indexopen: 2-5, 13, 21, 29, 37, 45; Christie's Images/CORBIS: 4; istockphoto: 5; Shutterstock: 5, 13, 29, 45, 47; The Granger Collection, New York: 21, 37; Bettmann/CORBIS: 46

FIRE MOUNTAIN

Written by
GLEN DOWNEY

Illustrated by
LIAM THURSTON

CHARACTERS

REAL PEOPLE IN HISTORY

PLINY THE ELDER (23-79 C.E.): He was a commander of the Roman navy and a scientist who studied nature.

PLINY THE YOUNGER (62-113 C.E.): Pliny the Elder's nephew. He was only 17 years old at the time of the eruption.

POMPONIANUS (dates unknown): A friend of Pliny the Elder.

FICTIONAL CHARACTERS

CATO: A 10-year-old slave boy from the city of Pompeii.

MINERVA: Cato's mother.

STEPHANUS: The slave master of Cato and Minerva.

DIANA: A 12-year-old slave girl from Pompeii who becomes Cato's friend.

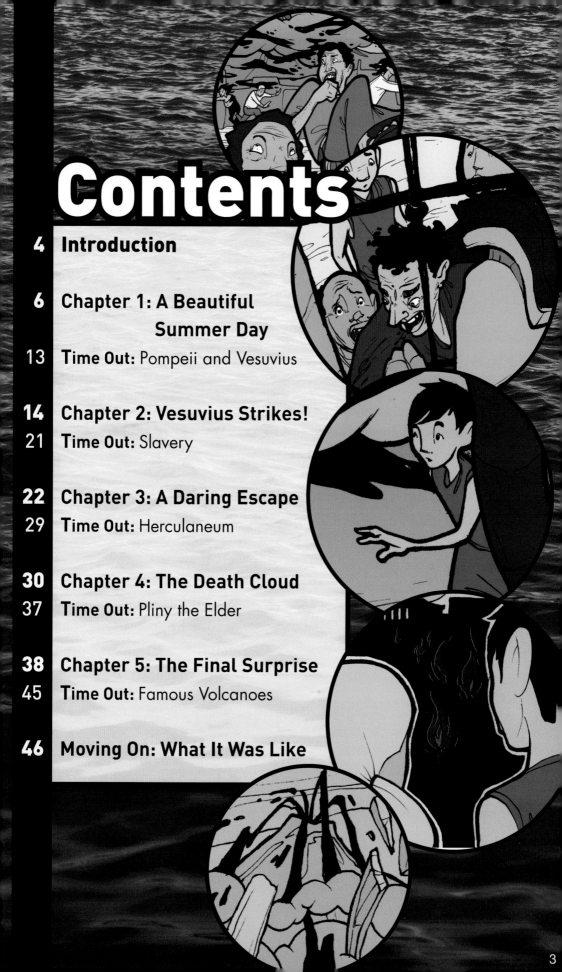

Contents

THOUSANDS FLEE SUMATRA VOLCANO
BBC News, April 13, 2005

VOLCANO ERUPTS, COVERS COLOMBIA IN ASH
Associated Press, November 24, 2005

ERUPTIONS PUT ALASKANS ON VOLCANO ALERT
Associated Press, January 15, 2006

Today, we can read and hear news about volcanic activities as soon as they happen in any part of the world. We can also get information and images of volcanic eruptions over the Internet.

TIMELINE

The letters B.C.E. stand for "Before Common Era." The years before the Common Era are counted backwards, so the greater the number, the longer ago it was. For example, 89 B.C.E. is farther in the past than 23 B.C.E.

600 B.C.E. »	89 B.C.E. »	23 C.E. »	62 C.E. »
The town of Pompeii, located southeast of Naples, Italy, is founded.	Pompeii becomes an important port for goods going to Rome or southern Italy.	Pliny the Elder is born in Como, Italy.	Pliny's nephew, Pliny the Younger, is born. In this year, a series of earthquakes rocks Pompeii, damaging several buildings.

We know how volcanoes work. Deep under the Earth's crust is molten (melted) rock called magma. As magma cools, it gives off gases and builds up pressure. When the pressure becomes too great, the magma and its gases break through a weak spot in a mountain, and a volcanic eruption takes place.

Volcanic eruptions can give off poisonous gases and spew out hot, molten rocks. They can also cause earthquakes and landslides.

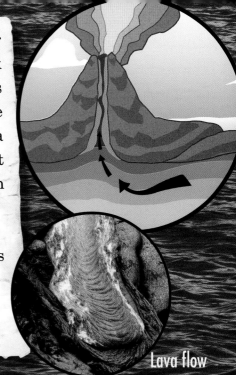

Lava flow

Ruins of Pompeii

On August 24 in 79 C.E., a huge volcanic eruption occurred in the beautiful Bay of Naples in Italy. The volcano was Vesuvius, and the eruption was the first in history to be recorded in detail. This story is about Vesuvius and what happened when this fire mountain roared!

WHAT'S THE STORY? This story is set in an actual time in history and depicts real people, but some of the characters and events are fictitious.

79 C.E. 》	79 C.E. 》	113 C.E. 》	1738 C.E.》	1748 C.E.》
On August 24, Mount Vesuvius erupts, burying Pompeii, Herculaneum, and other surrounding towns.	On August 26, Pliny the Elder is found dead on the beach at Stabiae.	Pliny the Younger dies.	Archeologists start excavating the ruins of Herculaneum.	Archeologists start excavating the ruins of Pompeii.

IT'S JUST PAST NOON ON A BEAUTIFUL DAY IN THE CITY OF POMPEII.

THE TOWNSPEOPLE GO ABOUT THEIR BUSINESS.

CATO, A YOUNG SLAVE, TAKES HIS MASTER'S CLOTHES TO BE CLEANED.

THE MOUNTAIN RUMBLES.

CATO!

CATO! WHAT'S WRONG?

I THINK I'VE TWISTED MY ANKLE. IT HURTS!

Buildings of Pompeii

POMPEII AND VESUVIUS

Pompeii was an ancient Roman colony and an important city for trade. It was known for its wines and perfumes. Many wealthy Romans spent their vacations there.

Close to the city of Pompeii stood Mount Vesuvius, a volcano. This area was frequently jolted by large earthquakes.

A bad earthquake hit Pompeii in 62 C.E., damaging several buildings. In 79 C.E., a disastrous eruption occurred. It buried the towns of Herculaneum and Pompeii.

ITALY

Pompeii

SLAVERY

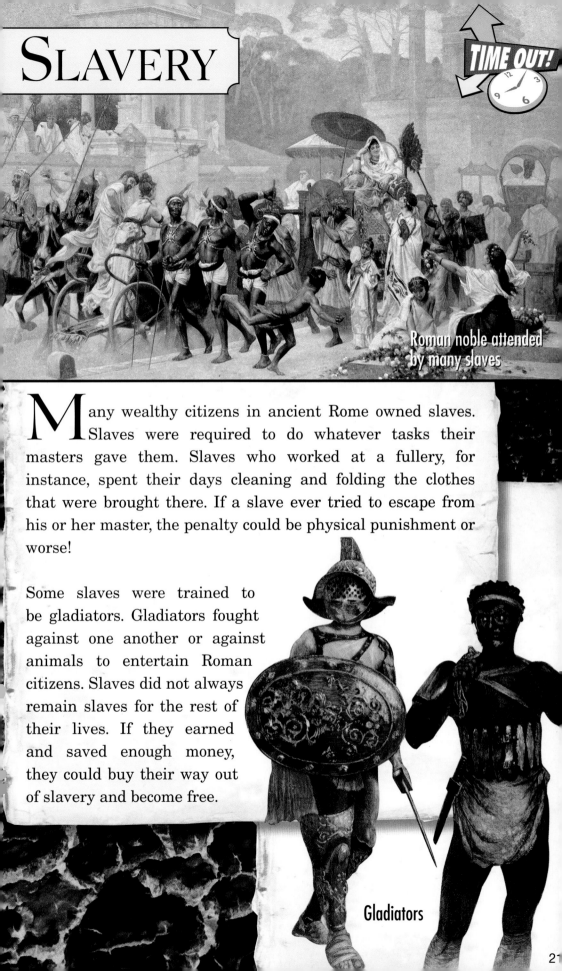

Roman noble attended by many slaves

Many wealthy citizens in ancient Rome owned slaves. Slaves were required to do whatever tasks their masters gave them. Slaves who worked at a fullery, for instance, spent their days cleaning and folding the clothes that were brought there. If a slave ever tried to escape from his or her master, the penalty could be physical punishment or worse!

Some slaves were trained to be gladiators. Gladiators fought against one another or against animals to entertain Roman citizens. Slaves did not always remain slaves for the rest of their lives. If they earned and saved enough money, they could buy their way out of slavery and become free.

Gladiators

CATO HAS A PLAN.

I'M SMALL ... THEY WON'T SEE ME.

HOLD YOUR TONGUE, CITIZEN!

YOU'LL DO AS WE SAY, OR ELSE...

LET US THROUGH!

IT'S NOW OR NEVER.

HERCULANEUM

Herculaneum was an ancient Roman town that was smaller but wealthier than Pompeii. It was located to the north and west of Pompeii and to the west of Vesuvius.

When the mountain began to rumble at 1:00 P.M. on August 24, many citizens of Herculaneum went down to the beach. They hoped to be rescued or to take shelter in the boathouses.

The next eruption occurred on the morning of August 25. It took only four minutes for the hot ashes to reach Herculaneum and bury the people on the shore.

Some of the remains of the residents of Herculaneum were not discovered until 1982, more than 1,900 years after the eruption.

BUT THERE IS NO REST FOR THE MOUNTAIN.

THE MOUNTAIN ONCE AGAIN SENDS ITS FIERY SURGE ON HERCULANEUM, BURNING EVERYTHING IN ITS PATH AND BOILING THE SEA.

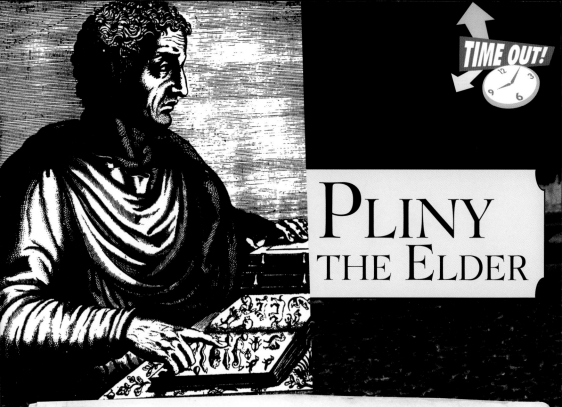

PLINY
THE ELDER

P liny the Elder was a scientist and a commander in the Roman navy. When he heard about the eruption of Vesuvius, he set out to help. His ship could not land at Pompeii, which had been hit by the eruption, so he chose the port of Stabiae. Then Stabiae was also hit. Pliny the Elder, like many others, died on the shore at Stabiae.

Pliny's nephew, Pliny the Younger, recorded the eruption of Vesuvius and his uncle's brave actions.

... Now came the dust, though still thinly. I looked back: a dense cloud loomed behind us, following us like a flood poured across the land.

... We had scarcely sat down when a darkness came that was not like a moonless or cloudy night, but more like the black of closed and unlighted rooms. You could hear women lamenting, children crying, men shouting.

... It grew lighter, though that seemed not a return of day, but a sign that the fire was approaching. The fire itself actually stopped some distance away, but darkness and ashes came again, a great weight of them. ...

Without the young Pliny's letters, we would know very little about what happened that day.

HELP!

RUN!

THE SURGE CLOUD HAS NEARLY RUN OUT OF ENERGY...

... BUT ITS TOXIC FUMES ARE STILL POWERFUL.

QUICK, JUMP!

FAMOUS VOLCANOES

The eruption of Vesuvius in 79 C.E. made it one of the world's most famous volcanoes. Here are some others:

- **World's Biggest Volcano**: Mauna Loa in Hawaii. Also the biggest mountain on the planet, Mauna Loa is 10.5 miles high from its base on the seafloor. It covers an area of 2,000 square miles and has a volume of 19,193 cubic miles!

- **Longest-Lasting Eruption**: It's still going on! Mount Kilauea in Hawaii has been erupting since 1983.

- **Most Powerful Eruption in History**: Mount Tambora in Indonesia in 1815. This eruption threw so much dust into the air that world temperatures were lowered by 5 degrees Fahrenheit. It was the deadliest volcanic eruption ever, killing 92,000 people.

- **Largest Volcanic Landslide**: Mount St. Helens, Washington. The eruption in 1980 triggered a landslide that was 22 square miles in area. About 3.7 billion cubic yards of rock debris rushed down the mountainside at 155 mph.

Plaster casts of people killed in eruptions of Vesuvius

For many centuries, Pompeii and Herculaneum were forgotten. Then, as archaeologists began to dig in the 16th century, they discovered the cities that were buried so many years ago.

WAS LIKE

The eruption happened so quickly that people were killed as they were going about their normal lives. Herculaneum was destroyed by burning ash and toxic gas. A steady rain of ash and rock fell over Pompeii and covered the city, killing thousands of people.

The hot ash that had buried the bodies turned into solid rock. As the bodies decomposed, they left holes in the rock. Archeologists have filled these holes with plaster and created casts of people and animals killed that day. They have also dug out streets and buildings, as well as markets, temples, public baths, and gardens.

Vesuvius has erupted dozens of times since 79 C.E. It could strike again at any moment. This is scary because thousands of people live and work near the mountain today.

Ruins of Pompeii

INDEX